It goes like this -

Fortunately

*
*

Things exist.

There could be nothing everywhere.

But everything is where it is.

*

Things also happen.

My Life could have never begun.

But it did.

*

Things can change.

My Life could be over this instant.

But it's not.

*
*

I have time

*
*

My time is my time.

It's already mine.

I can do with it as I please.

*

I am my own entity.

I can take my time.

I can do what pleases me.

*

I can try to appreciate the time I have.

I don't have to.

I'm free.

*

I don't have to do anything.

Neither does anyone else.

*

Every one of us is already free.

None of us even have to believe it.

*
*

Us

*
*

We are the living.

We live here.

*

All of us do.

For the time being -

We are alive.

*

This is us.

Our time is now.

*

We are phenomenal.

Life can be hard to believe.

All of us were once a single cell.

*

We've come a long way.

Here we are.

*

We're still going.

Here we go.

*
*

We can go peacefully

*
*

We're here already.

We can accept it.

*

We are what we are.

We have the ability to accept what we are.

Any one of us can do it.

*

One of us is me.

When I'm being honest about what I am -

I can accept what I am.

*

I can be honest.

All by myself -

I can.

*

Honestly -

I can make peace with what I am.

*
*

Right now

*

*

What I am is here.

Please allow me to introduce myself.

*

I'm me.

The one and only -

*

I'm the one that can be honest with myself.

When I notice that I haven't been -

I can give myself credit for noticing.

*

What I notice is what I notice.

When I notice anything -

I'm the one doing the noticing.

*

This is me.

I can interpret what I notice however I want.

*

*

Everything is open to reinterpretation

*

*

The history of human thought is a work in progress.

We're making this up as we go along.

Every thought was once a new thought.

*

Thoughts are thoughts.

Everything else is everything else.

*

Thoughts happen in the mind.

Everything else happens everywhere else.

*

I have my own mind.

My thoughts are the ones happening inside it.

I'm the one thinking my thoughts.

*

My mind is flexible.

What I think now can be different than what I thought before.

*

No matter what I think -

I can change my mind.

*

*

I can

*
*

I have abilities.

I'm able to do things.

*

I can do anything I'm able to do.

My abilities are my own.

I can do whatever I can.

*

I can do no more than I can.

My abilities are limited.

I can only do what I am able to do.

*

My abilities' limits are flexible.

I have the ability to become more able.

*

I may be more able than I am aware.

I may have abilities I have yet to discover.

I can find out.

*
*

Discovery

*
*

I have the ability to learn.

When I'm willing to try -

I can do things I've never done before.

*

What I try to do is up to me.

I'm the one making my attempts.

*

I make them myself.

When I do -

*

My attempts may succeed.

And my attempts may fail.

*

Regardless of how they turn out -

As long as I'm here -

I can make new ones.

*
*

Clarity

*

*

I can be discerning.

I have the ability to differentiate.

I can tell one thing from another.

*

I can be confused.

I have the ability to make mistakes.

I can confuse one thing with another.

*

Without even trying -

I can confuse what is happening outside my mind with my thoughts.

I can forget that they are two different things.

*

I can remember.

I can differentiate what is happening in my mind from everything else.

I can tell the difference.

*

I can be clear.

I don't have to confuse one thing with another.

I can see things for what they are.

*

*

Things are what they are

*
*

I can try to remember.

What is is.

What was was.

*

What is happening is happening.

What happened did.

*

That was then.

This is now.

*

Everything is what it is now.

Everything is where it is now.

Everything includes me.

*

Here I am.

I am what I am now.

*

I'm reading these words.

This is me.

*
*

Breaking the spell

*

*

I couldn't always read.

Now I can.

*

The alphabet is a tool I learned how to use.

I'm using it now.

*

The alphabet is a set of symbols that represent sounds.

These symbols, called letters, are used to make up words.

Words are standardized sounds that represent other things.

*

Some words represent things that exist.

Some words represent things that happen.

And some words represent things people imagine.

*

All words are made up.

No matter what anybody says -

Words are all anybody ever says.

*

Words are words.

Words are not the things they represent.

I can tell the difference.

*

*

Credence

*
*

Anybody can tell anybody anything with words.

And anybody can believe them.

*

I can believe what anybody tells me.

And I can believe what I tell myself.

*

My mind is impressionable.

I can be convinced that anything is true.

*

No matter what I believe -

I'm the one believing it.

While I do -

*

What I believe is what I believe.

What people say is what people say.

What is happening is what is happening.

*

I'm clear.

I can tell the difference.

*
*

Utility

*
*

There are rules for using words.

Obedience is optional.

*

How I use words is up to me.

I have options.

*

I can keep my mind clear.

When I use words -

I don't have to misrepresent anything.

*

I can be sincere.

When I use words -

I can say what I mean.

*

It's up to me.

When I want to represent myself accurately -

I can use words that affirm what I am.

*

As long as I'm here -

I always can.

*
*

I am here

*
*

This here is me.

I exist.

*

I don't have to think about it.

My existence requires no explanation.

It just is.

*

Here I am.

No matter what I tell myself I am -

All of me is here now.

*

Words can't make me any more or less here.

I am already here completely.

*

I am whole.

I am self-contained.

I have integrity.

*

I don't have to say a word.

I can just be.

I already am.

*
*

Really

*
*

I'm breathing.

I wouldn't be here otherwise.

*

I have my own breath.

It goes in and out of me.

*

I breathe automatically.

When I choose to, I breath intentionally.

Either way, I'm the one doing the breathing.

*

I'm still doing it.

I'm still here.

I've survived.

*

Here I am.

This is me.

I'm alive.

*
*

The opportunity of a Lifetime

*
*

Life was here before me.

I emerged from It.

*

I was born.

Now I'm here.

*

This is the Life I've got.

It's already mine.

I'm the one that gets to live it.

*

I get to be alive.

I get to be here now.

I get to be free.

*

I get to live This Life.

I get to have this experience.

I get to be me.

*
*

Temporarily

*

*

I won't be here forever.

Being alive is a limited time experience.

This Life is a temporary endeavor.

*

All lives end.

This Life will end too.

*

It could end without warning.

I'm here until it does.

*

I'm still here.

This Life didn't end.

It's not over yet.

*

For the time being -

This Life continues.

*

*

Voluntarily

*

*

This Life doesn't have to continue.

I'm here already.

I'm not obligated to be here any longer.

*

I can choose to leave.

For now -

I can choose to stay.

*

At the moment -

I have options.

*

I can give up my time here.

Or I can continue to spend it.

*

I can decide to live This Life.

Or I can end it.

*

The choice is mine.

This Life is free.

What I do with it is up to me.

*

*

Individually

*

*

This Life is singular.

It is what it is.

I don't have to confuse it with anything else.

*

I am This Life.

There's only one of me.

I am what I am myself.

*

My mind is mine alone.

I can try using it.

Honestly -

*

Right now -

This Life is what I happen to be.

*

No matter what I think I am -

The one doing the thinking is me.

*

*

Re-affirming

*

*

I live here.

As long as I continue to breathe -

I do.

*

I can believe it.

I can disbelieve it.

I'm here either way.

*

Like the rest of us -

I'm one of us too.

*

I'm this one.

Here I am.

*

This one of us is me.

Here I go.

*

*

I go with everything

*
*

I'm me.

Everything else is everything else.

Me and everything else is everything.

*

Everything is all that there is.

It just is.

Nothing else exists.

*

In this moment -

Everything is occupying it's own space.

Simultaneously -

*

Here This Life is now.

Along with everything else -

I'm a part of everything.

*
*

Humility

*
*

I am not everything.

I'm just me.

*

I am not all that there is.

I am all that I am.

*

I don't have to think that I'm more than I am.

I don't have to think that I'm less.

*

I can be self-aware.

When I'm being honest about myself -

*

I have clear boundaries.

I can tell the difference between me and everything else.

*
*

Ownership

*
*

This Life had its own beginning.

It will have its own end.

*

I'm here now.

Embodied consciously -

*

I have my own flesh.

I have my form.

*

I occupy my own space.

I am my own entity.

*

This Life is self-possessed.

I belong to no one else.

*

The experience I'm having is my own.

I don't have to try to put it into words.

*

Non-verbally -

My presence speaks for itself.

*
*

Acknowledgment

*

*

I've always been me.

I don't know what it's like to be anything else.

I can only imagine.

*

My mind is powerful.

I can imagine anything imaginable.

*

I can even imagine that what I'm imagining is actual.

Or I can acknowledge that it's just my imagination.

*

I can remain clear.

I don't have to confuse myself with my mind.

*

I can try to remember -

I am not what is happening inside it.

*

No matter what I think -

I can acknowledge that thoughts are all I ever think.

*

*

This Life is a sight to behold

*

*

What I am is visible.

It doesn't have to be a mystery.

*

What I am is here.

I have eyes.

I can see.

*

When I want to -

I can look at what I am.

*

When I do -

I don't have to confuse what I'm seeing with ideas I have about me.

*

I can believe my eyes.

No matter what I think I might be -

*

When I look at what I am -

I can see me.

*

*

To see or not to see

*
*

I can choose to see myself.

And I can choose not to.

Both options are available to me.

*

At the moment -

I have the ability to take-in visual information.

And I have the ability to keep it out.

*

My eyes have lids.

I don't have to see a thing.

*

I can hold my eyes shut for as long as I want.

And I can open them whenever I please.

*

My eyes are mine.

Opening them or not is up to me.

*
*

Independently

*

*

I am free.

What I choose to do and how I choose to do it depends on me.

*

I have options.

I have the ability to make a choice.

I can act deliberately.

*

I get to decide which of my options I will choose.

And which I won't -

*

It's up to me.

Choosing is optional.

*

I don't have to make choices.

I can also just do things.

Spontaneously -

*

*

Adaptability

*
*

This Life is self-operating.

My behavior is my own.

Entirely -

*

No matter what I'm doing -

I'm the one doing it.

Yes, me -

*

I have my own will.

I am my own authority.

I have the ability to change my behavior myself.

*

I'm already doing what I'm doing now.

When I remember that I have other options -

I can choose to do something else.

*
*

I'm already reading these words

*
*

I can choose to continue.

I can choose to stop.

Both options are available to me.

*

At the moment, I've chosen to continue.

Or, I'm continuing out of habit.

Both are possibilities.

*

The more I do habitually, the less I do by choice.

Either way, the one doing the doing is me.

*

My behavior is mine.

Whether I've chosen it or not -

*

I'm the one that can change it.

Instantaneously -

*
*

Now's my chance

*
*

What happened already did.

This moment is new.

Continuously -

*

It wasn't here before.

Now it is.

*

Again and again -

This moment is a new opportunity.

*

I can take it or leave it.

I can do something now or not.

It's up to me.

*

Beyond this moment -

I can't do a thing.

*

Now I can.

Indefinitely -

*
*

Here are my options

*
*

They are where I am now.

Wherever I happen to be -

My options are here too.

*

My options are limited.

Beyond my present location -

There's nothing I can do.

*

Here there is.

Here I am.

*

Regardless of what I did elsewhere -

I have options here still.

*
*

I always have a choice

*
*

My options vary.

Some that are here now won't be here later.

Others will be here later that aren't here now.

*

Some options come along once in a Lifetime.

Outside of my imagination, others never do.

And some options are here all the time.

*

For example -

Considering my options is always an option of mine.

*

I can always ask myself -

Do I really want to do what I'm about to do -

Or is not doing it a better option for me?

*

It may take all the courage I have -

But I can trust myself enough to answer.

Honestly -

*
*

I can do what I want

*
*

I have my own desire.

When I want to do something -

I'm the one that wants to do it.

*

My desire is a sensation that I feel.

It arises in me.

I feel it when I do.

*

What I feel is what I feel.

My sensations don't have to make any sense.

They're just what I'm feeling.

*

When I feel like doing something -

I can attempt to do it.

Or I can restrain myself.

*

I am my own authority.

When I follow my desire depends on me.

And no one else -

*
*

Self-control

*
*

I don't always know what I want to do.

Sometimes I'm not aware of it yet.

*

I can relax.

I don't have to do anything right now.

I'm free, even if I forget.

*

I don't have to act any particular way.

I don't have to think that I'm supposed to.

*

I have no obligations.

I'm not obligated to imagine that I do.

*

I have options.

I get to make my own choices.

Everything else is out of my control.

*

I'm just in charge of me.

I can only do what I can.

Whenever I please -

*
*

I can speak

*
*

I have my own voice.

I can say whatever I want.

In whatever manner I please -

*

Words can be powerful tools.

Aloud and in my mind -

I can use them intentionally.

*

To myself and others -

What I choose to say is up to me.

So is how I say it.

*

I can raise or lower my voice.

When I use words -

I can also change the pace and tone of my speech.

*
*

I can remain silent

*
*

I can say one thing one moment and something different the next.

I can say the same thing over and over again.

Or I can say nothing at all.

*

It's up to me.

I have the ability to be quiet.

Immediately -

*

No matter what I'm saying -

Aloud or in my mind -

I can stop saying it.

*

I learned to use words.

I didn't always know how.

I don't have to use them now.

*

When I notice that I am -

I could just stop.

*
*

I can be attentive

*
*

What is happening is happening.

It already is.

*

Whether I'm aware of it or not -

What is happening is happening anyway.

*

I don't have to ignore it.

I have my own attention.

I can observe what is happening for myself.

*

In this moment -

I can give my attention to what is happening in my mind.

Or I can give my attention to what is happening somewhere else.

*

My attention is mine to give freely.

What I do with it is up to me.

*
*

I can refocus

*
*

My attention can wander on its own.

Or I can control it.

Willfully -

*

I can ask myself -

Right now -

Is my attention where I want it to be?

*

When I want to know I can answer.

Honestly -

*

Nothing is entitled to my attention.

I get to decide what I'll give it to myself.

*

Regardless of where it is now -

I can choose to give it to something else.

*
*

I can come to my senses

*

*

When I take-in information -

I can be aware of what I'm doing.

*

When I give the information I'm receiving from my eyes my attention -

I can be aware of what I'm seeing.

*

When I give the information I'm receiving from my ears my attention -

I can be aware of what I'm hearing.

*

When I give the information I'm receiving from my nose my attention -

I can be aware of what I'm smelling.

*

When I give the information I'm receiving from my tongue my attention -

I can be aware of what I'm tasting.

*

When I give the information I'm receiving from my body my attention -

I can be aware of what I'm feeling.

*

And when I give my thoughts my attention -

I can be aware of what I'm thinking.

*

*

I can update what I think

*
*

Everything can't always be what it was.

Anything can change.

Instantaneously -

*

No matter what I thought things were before -

I can observe what they are now for myself.

*

When what I'm observing contradicts what I thought -

I can think something else.

*

I have the ability to reorganize my mind.

I can reconcile what I think with what I've observed.

At any time -

*

My thoughts and my observations don't have to stay misaligned.

What I think is open to improvement.

Giving things my attention and replacing old thoughts are options of mine.

*
*

I can know what I mean

*
*

When I use words -

What they mean to me is what they mean to me.

*

I'm the one using them.

When I do -

I can do so consciously.

*

Aloud and in my mind -

When I use words -

I can be aware of how I have them defined.

*

When I'm aware of what the words I'm using mean to me -

I can think and communicate self-confidently.

*

When I want to -

I can stop using words I can't clearly define.

I'll know what I mean when I do.

*
*

I can think freely

*
*

Thinking is optional.

It doesn't have to be a habit.

*

I can think when I want to.

And not when I don't -

*

My mind is mine.

Mastering it is up to me.

*

When I notice that I'm thinking without having chosen to -

I can discontinue the thought.

Repeatedly -

*

I can give my mind a break.

I don't have to contemplate anything right now.

*

For the moment -

I can just be here for being's sake.

*
*

My presence is enough

*

*

I don't have to deny it.

It's OK for me to exist.

I can accept that I do.

*

I'm already here.

Yes, me -

*

As a matter of fact -

I happen to exist.

Personally -

*

I don't have to take it for granted.

I can appreciate that I got to be here.

As long I continue to be -

*

*

Everything is acceptable

*
*

As it is -

In this moment -

*

Things are what they are.

I don't need them to be other than what they are.

*

Honestly -

The truth is acceptable to me.

I can handle it.

*

While something exists -

I can accept that it does.

*

When something ceases to exist -

I can accept that it doesn't.

*

And when I imagine that something exists -

I can accept that that's what I'm doing.

*
*

My ego

*
*

Doesn't actually exist.

But it can happen anytime.

*

It's when there's a discrepancy -

Between what I am and what I am in my mind.

*

My mind is a versatile tool.

How carefully I use it is up to me.

*

I don't have to think that I'm something I'm not.

I can conceive of myself accurately.

*

When I notice that I haven't been -

I can give myself respect for noticing.

*
*

I have my own respect

*
*

I can give it to whatever I want.

In this moment -

Everything's an option for me.

*

As long as I'm here -

I can try to regard anything, actual or imagined, positively.

*

I don't need reasons.

I can be generous.

My respect is free.

*

I don't have to withhold any of it ever.

From anyone or anything -

Including me -

*
*

Inclusivity

*
*

This Life is not all that is happening.

In this moment -

Everything else that is happening is happening too.

*

I'm alive.

Presently -

So are all of you.

*

We live here together.

I can accept that we do.

*

Here we all are.

Us includes everybody.

*

Regardless of what someone thinks they are -

I can consider them one of us too.

*
*

Making better decisions

*
*

Improves things for all of us.

Not just me -

*

Fortunately -

I don't have to wait for others to make better decisions.

I am my own authority.

*

I have my own intelligence.

I can use it faithfully.

*

When I make decisions -

I can choose what I believe is my best option.

Instead of doing something else -

*

I can be honest.

When I want things to improve -

I can trust myself.

*
*

I can be patient

*
*

Sometimes -

Things won't change.

That can be OK with me.

*

Everything is only what it is now.

I can just let it be.

*

Trying to appreciate things for what they are is an option.

I can choose it wholeheartedly.

*

This is my Life.

How I go about it is up to me.

*

I can take my time.

I can take another breath.

And I can remind myself that I'm still free.

*

The rest of This Life begins now.

Honestly -

What I do next is up to me.

*
*

ISBN-13: 978-0692348000 Poppy Reed Press
ISBN: 069234800X

www.letstryhonestly.com

Made in the USA
San Bernardino, CA
13 January 2015